"That slovenly fellow which you see before us...will be one of the greatest men of England." So wrote the English parliamentarian John Hampden about Oliver Cromwell in 1640.

Hampden was right. During the bitter and bloody struggles of the English Civil War, Cromwell rose from obscurity to become the shrewdest and most able military leader of the Roundheads. After Charles I's defeat he was the only man who could unite the quarrelling Parliament and Army. Indeed, his power and influence were so great that he was asked by Parliament to assume the title of King. After much wrestling with his conscience he refused, and instead took the title of Lord Protector. Thus the man who had sought the King's execution became king himself in all but name.

Amanda Purves tells the story of Cromwell's remarkable career as a distinguished military leader and as a rather less successful politician. She traces the development of the republic Cromwell fought so hard to establish and explains why he holds a key position in the study of English History.

More than fifty illustrations, glossary, list of principal characters, reading list, table of dates and index.

WAYLAND HISTORY MAKERS

Cromwell

Amanda Purves

WAYLAND PUBLISHERS LIMITED

More Wayland History Makers

The Wright Brothers Russell Ash
Martin Luther King Patricia Baker
Cecil Rhodes Neil Bates
Jomo Kenyatta Julian Friedmann
Rommel F. H. Gregory
Goering F. H. Gregory
Hitler Matthew Holden
Bismarck Richard Kisch
Lenin Lionel Kochan
Al Capone Mary Letts
Karl Marx Caroline Seaward
The Last Czar W. H. C. Smith
Picasso David Sweetman
Captain Scott David Sweetman
The Borgias David Sweetman
Franco Richard Kisch
Joseph Stalin David Hayes and F. H. Gregory
Mao Tse-tung Hugh Purcell

frontispiece: An engraving showing
Oliver Cromwell in a thoughtful
mood. The book on the table is
by the Dutch theologian Grotius.

SBN 85340 451 8
Copyright © 1977 by Wayland (Publishers) Ltd
First published in 1977 by Wayland (Publishers) Ltd
49 Lansdowne Place, Hove, East Sussex
Printed in Great Britain by Butler & Tanner Ltd
Frome and London

Contents

Introduction

Above Oliver Cromwell in Puritan dress, Bible in hand. From a Dutch engraving.

The years 1603–49 saw some of the most dramatic events in the whole of British history. During these forty-six years the position of the king as head of government was continually challenged by Parliament. The quarrel became so intense that it finally erupted onto the battlefield. From 1642–48 England was torn apart by bitter and bloody civil wars which eventually resulted in the execution of the King, Charles I, on 30th January, 1649.

England was then left in the unique position of having abolished the monarchy but with no clear form of government to turn to. The next eleven years, the period that is usually called either the Commonwealth or Interregnum, were years of great turmoil as the leaders of Parliament desperately tried to find a workable and popular form of government in which no one person held the reins of power.

But what caused this conflict between Charles I and his Parliament? It was not a sudden quarrel. The rumblings of discontent had been heard as far back as the end of Elizabeth I's reign in 1603. One of the main reasons was the desire of Parliament—particularly the House of Commons—to make itself indispensable to the king and thus play a more important role in governing the country. To achieve this aim it had to make itself equal in power—if not superior—to the king. During the years before the outbreak of the Civil War the leaders of the Commons sought to curb the King's power in every way they could, a policy which he naturally resented and opposed by trying to rule without them.

This already complicated and tense political situation was made even worse by the quarrels over religion which erupted at the same time. In the past, most religious disputes had been between Roman Catholics and Protestants. Now the friction came from within the Church of England itself. On one side stood the King and his supporters, who favoured an elaborate High Anglican form of church service and the government of the Church by bishops (the Episcopacy). On the other side was a group known as the Puritans, who sought to establish a purer, more simple form of religious worship. These Puritans who opposed the King in religious matters were often the same men who spoke out against him in Parliament.

The Puritan leaders were an extremely determined and active group of men. They won a great deal of support throughout England, particularly among the poor. The King and his supporters were equally stubborn and, as Charles tended to be rather tactless and outspoken in his views, the likelihood of any sort of agreement being reached between the two sides became more and more improbable.

It was during this turbulent period that a man emerged who was to change the face of history, a man who was to hasten the collapse of the monarchy and yet who was to become king himself in all but name. This man was Oliver Cromwell.

Below Charles I. His ornate clothes, earring and long hair contrast with Cromwell's simple dress. This engraving was copied from Lely's replica of Van Dyck's painting.

CROMWELL

Wale del.

Grignion Sculp.

1. I was by Birth a Gentleman

Oliver Cromwell is often remembered for his severe appearance, or because he was responsible for the execution of King Charles I. But what was this ugly, rather solemn man really like, and why is he so important in history?

Oliver Cromwell was born in the English town of Huntingdon on 25th April, 1599. His parents, Robert and Elizabeth, were typical country landowners of the time. His father was a Member of Parliament and a Justice of the Peace. They were fairly well off, and were connected by birth to some of the most influential families.

In 1604, when he was five, Oliver was sent to the Free School of Huntingdon. He was not an outstanding pupil but it was here, under the eye of his schoolmaster, Thomas Beard, that he was encouraged to take an interest in the Puritan religion. In 1616 he moved on to study at Sidney Sussex College, Cambridge, where he "perfectly acquired unto himself the Latin tongue". But most of his time seems to have been spent in "good fellowship and gaming". He did, however, become more interested in Puritanism, for Sidney Sussex was known for the Puritan bias of its teachers and was, according to Archbishop Laud, "a hotbed of Puritanism".

Oliver stayed at the University for only one year. In 1617 he had to return home because of the sudden death

"In the year of Our Lord 1599 the son of Robert Cromwell, gentleman, and Elizabeth, his wife, born the 25th day of April, and baptized on the 29th day of the same month."
The record of Cromwell's birth, still visible in the register of the Church of St John the Baptist, Huntingdon, England.

Opposite This engraving of Oliver Cromwell, with its fancy border, comes from Mountague's History of England.

> *Oliver Cromwell was sent to Sidney Sussex College, Cambridge,* **"more to satisfy his father's curiosity and desire, than out of any hopes of completing him his studies ... he was more interested in and famous for his Exercises in the Fields than in the schools ... being one of the chief matchmakers and players of Foot-ball, Cudgels or any other boysterous game or sport."** *He also spent his time* **"in uncontrolled debaucheries and publically declare[d] for Drinking, wenching and the outrages of licentious youth".**
> *The historian James Heath.*

> **"... look into those strange deep, troubled eyes of his, with their wild, murky sorrow and depth—on the whole wild face of his, a kind of murky chaos; almost a fright to weak nerves; to which nevertheless you look a second time ... and find it to be a thing the highest degree worth looking at."**
> *Thomas Carlyle on Cromwell.*

of his father. As the only surviving son among seven daughters, he had to comfort his mother and look after the family estates. A year later he "betook himself to study Law in Lincoln's Inn, that nothing be wanting to make him a complete gentleman and commonwealth man".

Left Cromwell House in Huntingdon High Street. The house was granted to the Cromwell family at the Dissolution of the Monasteries (1536) and is said to be Oliver Cromwell's birthplace.

It was during his time in London that Oliver fell in love with and eventually married Elizabeth Bouchier, the daughter of a wealthy London merchant. In 1620 he took his bride back to Huntingdon. Here they settled down to farming the estates and raising a family. Between 1620 and 1631 they had six children: Robert

Above Elizabeth, Oliver Cromwell's wife. They had eight children and a happy marriage.

(1621), Oliver (1623), Bridget (1624), Richard (1626), Henry (1628) and Elizabeth (1629). Two others were born later: Mary (1637) and Frances (1638). Theirs must have been a happy marriage, for thirty years later Oliver could still write to Elizabeth: "Truly I love thee not too well... thou art dearer to me than any other creature."

In 1628 the fortunes of the Cromwell family improved, for the death of a distant uncle enabled them to inherit some valuable property. Oliver was now a wealthy man and was important enough in his own district to be elected as a Member of Parliament for Huntingdon in Charles I's third Parliament, which was summoned in 1629. This Parliament was short and stormy, but during it Oliver made his maiden speech.

He had spoken during a rather heated debate on religion which was playing an increasingly large part in his life. Relations between Charles and Parliament had gone from bad to worse and, as a result, Charles dissolved Parliament after it had sat for only a few weeks. For the next eleven years Charles ruled without calling a Parliament. This period, 1629–40, is often called the Eleven Years' Tyranny.

There are several descriptions of Oliver's appearance at this time. The steward of his household says he was 5 ft 10 ins (1.78 m) tall, with a rugged appearance, blue eyes, an extra-long nose and a full, manly figure. In 1640 the Earl of Warwick wrote: "His stature was of good size... his countenance swollen and reddish, his voice sharp and irritable." His steward also says that he had "an exceedingly fiery temper". Occasionally Oliver suffered from terrible black moods of depression, which caused him to come out in a rash of boils. He could sometimes be seen wearing "a piece of red flannel, being subject to inflammation". He was also something of a hypochondriac and was terrified of catching the plague and other diseases which were then very common. He was often to be seen taking medicine.

As to his character, ever since he was very young, stories had circulated that there was something unusual about him. At his birth, the well-known astrologer, John Aubrey, predicted that he was to become "more eminent in his life than ordinary". At school Oliver had had visions of his future greatness and once described how "one appeared to him in the likeness of a man, who told him he should be king".

Apart from these occasional mystical flashes, Oliver seems to have been a fairly serious and normal young man. He loved "an innocent jest" and Richard Baxter says he "was naturally of such a vivacity and hilarity and alacrity as another man is when he hath drunken a cup of wine too much". He also enjoyed smoking tobacco, singing, dancing, hunting and fishing. Sir Philip Warwick writes that the "first years of [Oliver's] manhood [were] spent in a dissolute course of life, in good fellowship and gaming".

But by 1629 Oliver had become a straightforward, no-nonsense man whose main loves were his family, his religion and his estates. The best way of describing him is to use his own words: "I was by birth a gentleman, living neither in any height nor yet in obscurity...I endeavoured to discharge the duty of an honest man in those services to God and His people's interest and commonwealth." Thus, in a simple speech, Cromwell outlined his origins and aims as they were to remain for the rest of his life.

> **"He was grown ... so just and of so scrupulous a conscience that having some years before won thirty pounds off one Mr Carlton at play, meeting him accidentally, he desired him to come home with him and receive his money, telling him he had it by indirect means, and it would be a sin to him to detain it any longer."** *James Heath on Cromwell.*

2. Lord of the Fens

While England was growing restless under the "tyrannical" rule of Charles I, Cromwell was becoming involved in local politics. It was in this field that he started to make a name for himself, both in Huntingdon and further afield, in London.

In 1630 Cromwell was made Justice of the Peace for Huntingdon. This was an important office, for JPs had to make sure the laws passed in Parliament were actually carried out and obeyed. It was a job which was respected and one which automatically gave the holder a high position in country society. Cromwell took his job very seriously, unlike some of the other JPs. It was his keenness for his job which brought him into trouble with the Mayor of Huntingdon.

The Aldermen of the town had asked for a new charter. This was granted and by its terms the King had the right to choose the new Mayor. This upset the townspeople, who thought that the new Mayor would be nothing but a puppet in the hands of the King. Their complaint was taken up by Cromwell, who in the ensuing quarrel showed how strongly he felt about the denial of the people's right to choose their own Mayor. He was accused of making "disgraceful and unseemly speeches". His words were so violent that he was summoned to appear before the King's chief ministers, the Privy Council. Here, Oliver was persuaded to withdraw the words he had spoken in "heat and passion".

> **"None were more fond of a King than the English, yet they departed from him to ease their purses and consciences."** *Peter Chamberlayne, 1649.*

Opposite This triple portrait of Charles I was painted by Van Dyck in 1637 and sent to the Italian sculptor Bernini. Bernini thought Charles looked doomed and said he had never seen more unfortunate features. However, he made a bust of Charles which is now lost.

Above Ely and the River Ouse. Cromwell and his family lived in this fenland city for eleven years.

But the Mayor may have refused to accept his apology for, shortly afterwards, the Cromwells moved to St Ives.

This move saw a fall in their fortunes. Cromwell could not afford to buy his own farm and had to rent one. He even considered emigrating to America and starting a new life there. But in 1636 a wealthy uncle, Sir Thomas Seward, died and left Cromwell his estates in the nearby town of Ely. Once again the Cromwell family was on the move. They stayed in Ely for eleven years (1636–47) and it was there that Cromwell was recognized as being a man of wealth and importance.

At first Cromwell enjoyed a quiet life in his pleasant glebe cottage, which is still standing today. But this peaceful period was quickly shattered when Cromwell again became involved in a struggle between the local people and a royal command.

In 1634 Charles I ordered a company, under the direction of the Earl of Bedford, to drain the swampy fenlands around Ely and turn the area into grazing land. As a long-term policy it was a good one, but at the time it meant that many poor families would lose their livelihoods, as they relied on the Fens for their supplies of fish and game-birds. The Fenlanders showed their opposition to the King's orders by stoning the workmen and knocking down their buildings. From 1636–38 Cromwell took up their case and became their spokesman "in opposition to His Majesty's most commendable design". His intervention was successful and work had to be stopped. The Fens were eventually drained in 1653, but only after fairer terms had been agreed for the local people.

As a result of the leading role he played in the Fen dispute, Cromwell won much support and admiration. He was even nicknamed the "Lord of the Fens". But, more important, he had attracted the attention of the Puritan radicals in London. These men were the group who were becoming increasingly outspoken against Charles I and all that he stood for. They saw in Cromwell a possible ally. Their hopes were strengthened when they saw him support John Hampden rather than the King in the famous Ship Money Case. Also Cromwell openly supported the Scots in 1639 when they rebelled against Charles I after refusing to accept the Prayer Book that had been thrust on them by the King and the Archbishop of Canterbury, Archbishop Laud. The hopes of the Puritan radicals were to be justified.

In 1640, after a gap of eleven years, Charles I was finally forced to summon a parliament. He badly needed money to pay for what was called the First Bishops' War against Scotland. Failing to obtain

> **"It was commonly reported in Ely Fen adjoining, that Mr Cromwell had undertaken, they paying him a groat for every cow they had on common, to uphold the drainers in suit for five years, and in the meantime they should enjoy every foot of common."** *Report of 1638.*

Below William Laud, Archbishop of Canterbury, who opposed Puritans and Presbyterians. He was impeached by the Long Parliament in 1640, sent to the Tower, and executed in 1644 after a complicated trial.

> "The first time I ever took notice of him was in the beginning of the parliament held in November 1640, when I vainly thought my selfe a gentleman (for we courtiers vained ourselves much upon good clothes). I came one morning into the House well clad, and perceived a Gentleman speaking (whom I knew not). Very ordinarily apparelled: for it was a plain cloth-sute, which had seemed to have bin made by an ill country taylor; his linen was plain and not very clean; and I remembered a speck or two of blood on his little band, which was not much larger than his collar; his hatt was without a hatt-band; his stature was of good size, his sword struck close to his side; his countenance swolen and reddish, his voice sharp and untunable, and his eloquence full of fervour."
> *Sir William Warwick, writing of Cromwell.*

> "That slovenly fellow which you see before us, who hath no ornament in his speech; I say that sloven, if we should ever come to breach with the King (God forbid) in such case will be one of the greatest men of England."
> *John Hampden to Lord Digby, 1640.*

enough money from other sources, he turned to Parliament to grant him the funds. Cromwell was elected a Member of Parliament for Cambridge, and he immediately took his place at Westminster in what became known as the Short Parliament, because it lasted only three weeks (April–May 1640). The members refused to grant Charles any money until he had listened to their many complaints. But Charles was in no mood to listen and angrily dissolved Parliament. There are no records describing the part Cromwell played in this Parliament, but it is certain that he supported the majority of the MPs against the King.

In 1640 Cromwell was forty-one years old; in the seventeenth century this was considered to be well into middle-age. He had a loving family and was a competent farmer. He had made a significant impact in local government and was gaining a reputation for standing up for the rights of the common folk. He was also a devout Puritan. Sometime in the late 1620s and the early 1630s, Cromwell experienced a deeply moving spiritual re-awakening to Christianity. What exactly happened is not clear, but it was so powerful that for the rest of his life he never wavered from his deep and sincere religious beliefs. Whatever the situation or problem, on the battlefield or with Parliament, Cromwell always called on God for help and guidance.

He had now left behind him the high spirits of his youth. He was in a comfortable social position and was admired by many. At forty-one Cromwell was about to embark on what was to become a remarkable military and political career.

Right The House of Commons in the time of Charles I. The King is opening Parliament, and the Speaker is being presented to him.

Cancellarij Sedes v.

3. His Eloquence full of Fervour

The early months of 1640 were a time of great unrest. There were riots all over England. Many people refused to pay their rents and tithes (taxes paid to the church). But it was not only the common folk who were unhappy, for "men of mean and middling quality" were also becoming restless. The general feeling was that "the gentry have been our masters for a long time and now we may chance to master them." This attitude was also reflected in parliament. The Long Parliament (1640–60) was summoned in November 1640. It was called because Charles still needed financial aid for the Scots war.

Parliament assembled in a mood eager for action and reform. It was very critical, both of the King and of his policies. It disliked the Scots war and hated the King's "evil counsellors", whom they blamed for most of the troubles. These "evil counsellors" were Thomas Wentworth, 1st Earl of Strafford and the Archbishop of Canterbury, Archbishop Laud. Cromwell was typical of many MPs who sat in this Parliament. He was a wealthy landowner and he was related to eighteen other MPs, including John Hampden and Oliver St John. These two men brought Cromwell into the circle of the most powerful and radical man in the House of Commons—John Pym. Cromwell, therefore, found himself immediately "in" with the elite group. But he was also important in his own right. Out of all the MPs who

"When he first appeared in Parliament, he seemed to have a person in no degree gracious, no ornament of discourse, none of these talents which used to recruit the affections of standers-by [but] as he grew into place and authority his parts seemed to be renewed as if he had concealed faculties until he had occasion to use them." *Edward Hyde, 1st Earl of Clarendon, writing about Cromwell in his* History of the Great Rebellion.

Opposite The execution of Thomas Wentworth, Earl of Strafford, chief adviser to Charles I and lord-lieutenant of Ireland, at Tower Hill, 1641.

Gratious Soueraigne

Right Charles I greeted on his return to London from Scotland in 1641.

had sat in the Parliament of 1628, only a quarter were present in 1640. Cromwell was one of them and this experience gave him added prestige.

The new Parliament soon went into action. The MPs were determined to make sure that nothing like the Eleven Years' Tyranny could ever happen again. The Triennial Act was passed in order to make sure that a parliament would meet at least once every three years. Another Act stated that it could not be dissolved without its own consent. They also abolished Ship Money and other unpopular taxes. They forced Charles to sign the death warrant of the Earl of Strafford, who was nicknamed "Black Tom Tyrant". Archbishop Laud was imprisoned (he was eventually executed in 1645).

Cromwell was busy from the start. He supported Pym and his friends throughout the session and had a hand in framing the Triennial Act (it was he who demanded that it have a second reading). His activities and speeches brought him to the notice of Sir Philip Warwick. Although Warwick was at first struck by the

"The gentry who detesting a close, hardy and industrious way of living do eat bread in the sweat of other men, and were mostly Royalist."
Edmund Ludlow.

22

shabbiness of Cromwell's clothes he was soon won over by the greatness of his words.

It was in the area of religion that Cromwell was most concerned. He fiercely attacked the established Church in such a way that he gained the admiration of John Hampden. Cromwell was convinced of the "irregularities of Bishops". When Sir John Strangeways said "Bishops are one of the three estates of this kingdom," Cromwell completely lost his temper. His reply was so rude that a complaint was made about his "unparliamentary language". Although he disliked bishops, he confessed he did not know what he would rather have —"I can tell you what I would not have though I cannot what I would." He also wanted reforms in the Prayer Book, the spread of preaching and a simplification of the church service.

In the early days of this Parliament, Cromwell lost his temper on several occasions. He felt very strongly about certain issues and could not control his feelings. One of these issues was the old favourite—the Fen Dispute. This was brought up again in 1641. As before, Cromwell supported the Fenlanders. He was on the committee that was set up to deal with their complaints. He "ordered the witnesses and petitioners in the method of the proceedings; and seconded and enlarged upon what was said with great passion". At one point Cromwell thought the Chairman was against the Fenlanders. He became furious at their treatment. When a friend tried to calm him down, he answered with "so much indecency and rudeness" that no-one believed they were friends.

In the first six months of the Long Parliament, Cromwell was already in the foreground. He was a member of the select group which centred on John Pym, against the King. He was finding his feet and passionately expressing his views. But this was only a preview of what was to come.

Above John Pym, one of the five Members of Parliament Charles tried to arrest in 1642 and, according to Clarendon, "The most popular man and the most able to do hurt that hath lived in any time."

> **"You know what my manner of life hath been ... oh, I lived in darkness and hated light. I was a chief of sinners. This is true; I hated Godliness, yet God hath mercy on me."**
> *Cromwell in 1638.*

4. War without an Enemy

By October 1641 some of the more moderate MPs were rather wary of the reforms brought about by Pym and his friends. They felt that the reformers had gone too far and that too many ancient rights had been stolen from the King. This caused Charles I to become popular again for a brief time. But in the same month there was a serious rebellion in Ireland. Thousands of Protestants were reported to have been mercilessly butchered. Unfortunately, and quite unfairly, rumours went around that Charles was responsible. Both the King and his unhappy Parliament saw that the reconquering of Ireland was necessary. This brought up a very important question—who was to control the Army in Ireland?

By ancient right, the King was Commander-in-Chief of the Forces. By 1641, it was almost the only right that he had left. Pym had other ideas, for he was determined that Charles should not be in control of the Army. He was probably afraid that it might be used against himself and the other Puritan radicals in England.

In November, acting as the spokesman for the radicals, Cromwell presented the Grand Remonstrance to Charles. This was a long account (it had 204 clauses) of all the illegal or unconstitutional acts of Charles since the beginning of the reign. It also set out all the good work that Parliament had done, and demanded that all the King's ministers should be appointed by

> "Thou wouldst think it strange if I should tell thee there were time in England, when brothers killed brothers, cousins cousins ... and friends their friends ... when thou went to bed at night thou knewest not whether thou should be murdered afore day ... Sacrilege was a virtue, Sovereignty a high price for piety." *Sir John Oglander.*

Opposite The first act of the Civil War. The Governor of Hull refuses entry to the King.

Parliament. It was a sort of "vote of no confidence" in the King. There was a great struggle to get it passed, for many members felt that it was too extreme, and some feared that it would end in bloodshed. It was carried by a mere eleven votes. Pym had made sure that "no man of their party was absent". Cromwell was very much in favour of the Remonstrance. He told Lord Falkland later that if the Remonstrance had been rejected he would have sold all he had that morning and never have seen England more.

The Grand Remonstrance was followed by a Militia Bill which gave Parliament control of the armed forces. Charles was understandably furious at this turn of events. In his fury he attempted to arrest the five most powerful men in the House of Commons—Pym, Hampden, Holles, Strode and Haslerigg. He arrived in person at Westminster, accompanied by four hundred Cavaliers. But the five members had been forewarned. "The birds had flown."

The country was horrified by Charles's actions, for the King could only enter the House by invitation from the members. Thus his actions were seen as a serious breach of parliamentary privilege. Cromwell was by now

Below Charles demanding the arrest of the five members in the House of Commons, 1642.

aware that civil war could not be far off. He suggested that a committee be set up "to consider the means to put the kingdom in a posture of defence". Both the King and Parliament drew up plans of defence. Soldiers were recruited, forts and ports were secured. The Queen, Henrietta Maria, was ready to fight. She felt certain that her own country, France, would come to the aid of her husband. She even threatened to go into a nunnery if Charles did not show himself to be a man and fight. In February 1642 she sailed to Holland to pawn the Crown Jewels to pay for the war. She never returned to England again.

At the end of April 1642 Charles tried to enter the town of Hull. But the Governor closed the gates in the name of Parliament. This incident can be seen as the first act of the Civil War. In May, Charles issued a Proclamation which forbade troops to muster without his consent. This order went completely against the Militia Bill passed by Parliament the previous year. Parliament replied by releasing its Nineteen Propositions. This was a final attempt to find a peaceful solution. Charles refused to accept it as it would have made him nothing more than a puppet king. In August, Charles declared war.

In the summer of 1642 Cromwell left Ely to take part in "a war without an enemy". He had decided that war was the only way to solve the political and religious problems that were tearing the country in half. He felt it was his duty to fight for such a cause—a cause in which he firmly believed.

Cromwell on the eve of the Civil War was a very different man from the quiet but watchful MP of the Short Parliament. By the autumn of 1642 the rough, hot-headed farmer had risen to a place at the centre of the parliamentarian leadership. Respected, feared and admired, Cromwell prepared to wage war against his King.

> **"The war was begun in the streets before King or Parliament had any armies."** *Richard Baxter.*

> **"Your troops are most of them decayed serving men and tapsters and such odd fellows ... and their troops are gentlemen's sons and persons of quality ... you must get men of a spirit that is likely to go as far as gentlemen will go, or else be beaten yet."** *Cromwell remarking on John Hampden's troops, 1642.*

27

5. Divided Sovereignty

Once war had been officially declared, every Englishman had to make a painful decision. Was he to remain loyal and stand by the King? Or was he to become a rebel and support Parliament? It was a wretched choice. There were often differences between members of the same family, where father fought son and brother fought brother.

England was roughly divided into regional areas by the war. Broadly speaking, the Midlands, the North and the South-Western counties rallied round the King. The South-East and East Anglia supported Parliament. This meant that Parliament had the support of most of the wealthy areas of the country. More important, it also had London, which meant the control of all trade and the Fleet. In fact most of the large towns, except Oxford and Chester, supported Parliament.

To some extent, social class also decided which side a man fought for. "Gentlemen of ancient families [were] for the most part well-affected to the King." Those who supported Parliament were often "a people of inferior degree who, by good husbandry...had gotten large fortunes, some were gentry, divers of the inferior clergy, most of the tradesmen and very many of the peasantry". As far as numbers went, there was little to choose between the two sides. Very few of the recruits were actually trained soldiers. The general feeling at the beginning was that the "war" was really a bit of a game.

> **"There were few gentlemen and men of quality who were actively opposed to His Majesty."** *Clarendon*, History of the Great Rebellion.

Above This weapon, used by Cromwell's soldiers, is thought by some to have given Roundheads their name.

Opposite Cromwell in armour, painted by Robert Walker.

Opposite Prince Rupert charging at Edgehill. He was the son of the Elector Palatine Frederick V and Elizabeth, daughter of James I. His enthusiasm for action led to his nickname the "Mad Cavalier". After the war he became a buccaneer, fled to the West Indies, turned to scientific research, and improved the formula for gunpowder.

Surely no-one would really take up arms against their King?

On Parliament's side, the war was conducted through "the Committee of Lords and Commons for the Safety of the Kingdom". The Earl of Essex was their Commander-in-Chief. The Royalists operated through the Council of War, with the King as their leader. Both sides were given nicknames. The Royalists were known as "Cavaliers", which means "swash-buckling officers". The Parliamentarians were called "Roundheads", which means "crop-haired citizens".

At the start of the war, each MP tried to secure his county for the side that he had chosen to support. Cromwell was given orders to care for the safety of Cambridgeshire. He had to recruit trained soldiers and volunteers, and block bridges and ferries. Throughout the summer of 1642 he was busy organizing the defences in Cambridge. He also raised his own troop in Huntingdon. He arrested the Captain of the Cambridge troop, and stormed the castle. He also forced the University to surrender—but not without some fierce resistance from some of the colleges.

Cromwell's actions were important. Not only did he secure Cambridgeshire for Parliament, but he commanded some of the first actions of the war. The first major battle of the war took place in October 1642. The spot where the two armies met was at Edgehill, in Northamptonshire. The battle was bloody but there was no clear victory for either side. Cromwell had been amongst the men "of the right wing...who never stirred from their troops but fought till the last minute".

If Charles had chased after the Parliamentarian forces he might at this time have managed to capture London and end the war. Instead he spent the winter at Oxford, which gave the Roundheads time to recover. Nothing had been settled. Most men felt uneasy. But Cromwell had had his first taste of battle.

6. The Ironsides

By December 1642 East Anglia was almost entirely won for Parliament. The Eastern Association was set up to organize the troops in this part of the country. It was commanded by Edward Montagu, Earl of Manchester. Cromwell was on the committee which was responsible for all the Association's movements. He was also made a Colonel. In February 1643 his Huntingdon troop of Horse was made into a regiment. These men provided the core of what were to become the famous "Ironsides".

The new regiment first went into action about three months later. They defeated a Royalist party at Grantham, in Lincolnshire. This was the start of a Parliamentary campaign in the North and North-East. In July 1643 the siege of Gainsborough checked the Royalist advance. In this skirmish Cromwell was commended for his "discreet and valiant carriage". The final success in this campaign for the Ironsides was at Winceby, in Lincolnshire, in October. In this battle Cromwell's horse was shot dead from under him. But he mounted the nearest available animal and rallied his troops to victory. The battle of Winceby showed the spirit of Cromwell and his men. News of their courage spread, as did Cromwell's reputation for being a skilled commander.

What qualities made the Ironsides so extraordinary? First of all, Cromwell's "lovely troop" were carefully

"He [Cromwell] had special care to get religious men in his troop ... of greater understanding than common soldiers ... more apprehensive of the import of the war ... who were more engaged to be valiant ... it was the very esteem and love of the religious men that principally moved him; and the avoiding of those disorders, mutinies, plunderings and grievances of the country which [debauching] men in armies are commonly guilty of."
Richard Baxter on the Ironsides.

Opposite Soldiers leaving London to join Cromwell's army with hymns and prayers.

A Quadrant Fort with 4 Half Bulworks at Foxhall

Above The fort at Vauxhall, built during the Civil War. Behind the wall is the manor house, and in the distance Westminster Abbey and Lambeth Palace.

"A few honest men are better than numbers ... if you choose honest men to be captains of horse, honest men will follow them, and they will be careful to mount such." *Cromwell, 1643, on the Ironsides.*

recruited and trained. The men were chosen for their spirit, conscience and religion. Cromwell only picked "godly men" who "on a matter of conscience engaged upon this quarrel". Most remarkable was his choice of officers. It was the custom to choose gentlemen or men of high birth to be commanders. Instead Cromwell picked his officers according to their ability, character and skill. He was not worried about their social rank. Like himself, they were mostly amateurs who learned the finer points of war and battle as they went along.

Cromwell's troops were fed, clothed, armed and paid regularly. They were paid 2s 6d (12½p) a day, even if it meant that the money had to come from his own pocket. High standards were enforced by harsh discipline and rigorous training. An article in a newspaper of 1643 tells how "no mans swears, but he pays 12d (5p),

Left An engraving of the famous Van Dyck portrait of Cromwell.

if he be drunk he is set in the stocks or worse...how happy be it if all forces were thus disciplined." Public whippings were a common sight.

Cromwell's methods were new and so they were often criticized. However, many admired them and they certainly seem to have worked. Not only were his men good soldiers but Cromwell boasted that they were "the freest from unjust practices of any in England". A modern historian, Maurice Ashley, writes that, "the choice of spirited volunteers, sternness of discipline, care of personal needs and punctuality of pay...were the makings of the Ironsides."

Parliament was well pleased with the successes of Cromwell and his Ironsides after the campaign of 1643. So much so that he was rewarded by being made Governor of Ely.

7. Laurels of Fame and Honour

The winter of 1643–44 brought a dramatic change in Parliament's war policy. In November 1643 a treaty was signed between the Scots and Parliament. This was known as the Solemn League and Covenant. It stated that in return for £100,000, the Scots would send an Army to help Parliament in the Civil War. It also demanded that when the war was won, England would adopt the Presbyterian religion. Scottish help was on the whole welcomed, but many were reluctant to sign the Covenant, for they were afraid of the rigid system of the Presbyterians. (The Presbyterians were so called because they were governed by Presbyters, or Elders, and not by Bishops.) This hesitation caused a split among the Puritans. The two groups which appeared were known as the Presbyterians (those who supported all the clauses of the Covenant) and the Independents (those who favoured Scots help but wanted a less organized religious system). Cromwell belonged to the latter group. Scots help was too valuable to lose, so all signed the agreement. But the final document was cunningly worded so that England did not actually promise to become Presbyterian. Instead she merely promised to support the "best reformed churches".

As there was a split in Parliament over religion, so there was another developing as to how the war should be fought. On one side there were those who still thought it indecent to fight against the King. These were

> *Manchester:* **"If we beat the King nine times yet he is still King ... but if the King beats us but once, we shall all be hanged, and our posterity be made slaves."** *Cromwell:* **"My Lord, if this be so, why did we take up arms in the first place?"** *Conversation between the Earl of Manchester and Oliver Cromwell, 1644.*

Opposite After the Battle of Naseby, Cromwell fought against individual Royalist strongholds. Here a mansion is being enthusiastically sacked.

A Covenanting Scot & an Englifh Independent differ about y things of this
world

Above A satirical playing card, showing a Puritan and a Presbyterian disagreeing.

"We came down the hill in the bravest order ... and with the greatest resolution that was ever seen ... Cromwell's own division had a hard time of it, for they were charged by Rupert's bravest men, both in front and rank."
Cromwell's scout master on Marston Moor, 1644.

usually men of high rank who followed Presbyterianism. On the other side were those who wanted to win the war at all costs. These men were usually Independents who wished to see the monarchy overthrown and a republic established in its place.

Cromwell emerged as the leader of the "win the war" party. He was very eager to bring the war to a speedy and positive ending with a victory for Parliament. This brought him to a collision with the commander of Parliament's troops, the Earl of Manchester, who was still reluctant to fight Charles I. Cromwell angrily accused him of being half-hearted in his pursuit of the war.

Before this quarrel could develop any further, the Battle of Marston Moor took place. It was fought in July 1644, and was a resounding victory for Parliament. The Royalists had been completely surprised by the attack—their Commanders were just sitting down to dinner! In the heat of the battle, Cromwell received an injury in his neck. Undaunted, he roused his men to victory. It was this battle that won for Cromwell his reputation for being an extraordinary military commander. He was "crowned with never-withering laurels of fame and honour".

After Marston Moor, the quarrel between Cromwell and Manchester came to a head. Cromwell accused Manchester of not having taken full advantage of their success at Marston Moor. He believed that further attacks might have ended the war there and then. Cromwell also started to criticize the Solemn League and Covenant. By doing so he upset Manchester's supporters, the Presbyterians and the Scots. Hoping to ease the situation, Manchester sent troops down to the South-West, where the Parliamentary forces had been in some trouble. On the way down he ill-managed the second battle of Newbury (October 1644). Cromwell was furious, for once again he felt that they had missed a good chance to end the war.

However, Cromwell had a solution. It was incredible but effective. He said that "in a time of crisis, quarrels between commanders should be shelved for the more effective running of the war." He decided that the only way was to get rid of all the officers who were only half-heartedly commanding the war. To do this the Independents passed the Self-denying Ordinance in April 1645. This compelled all MPs and Peers to resign their commissions in the Army within forty days. Thus it removed all the men who owed their command to social rank rather than ability. There were exemptions (as in the case of Cromwell and Fairfax) and it did not prevent re-appointments.

The army was then re-organized by Cromwell on the plan of his Ironsides into what became known as the New Model Army. Its Commander-in-Chief was Sir Thomas Fairfax (1612–71). It had a total of 22,000 men—most of them coming from the Eastern Association. It was in fact the foundation of a large standing army, and its ranks were filled with "men of religion, who would", as Cromwell said, "withstand the gentlemen of honour of the Royalist army". Cromwell was made a Lieutenant-General. The Royalists rather rudely nicknamed it "The New Noddle Army".

Although at first it was severely criticized, the New Model Army was quietly given the chance to show its value. The Battle of Naseby (June 1645) was a great victory for Parliament and settled the outcome of the First Civil War. A Scottish commander described the battle thus: "Rupert in his fury pushes too far; Cromwell comes on the back of the King's Foot and Fairfax on their faces and quickly makes them lay down their arms". Over eight thousand Royalists were either killed or captured, while Parliament claimed to have lost only two hundred.

It was a truly shattering victory. Cromwell was full

"Picture ... the long line of horsemen with their breastplates glittering in the afternoon sun ... the solid mass of shouldered pikes ... the hundreds of fluttering pennants above them all, of all shapes and colours. The standard of Prince Rupert with its red cross, was nearly five foot long." *Sir Charles Markham on the Battle of Marston Moor.*

"Truly England and the Church of God had a great favour from the Lord; in this great victory given unto us, such as the like was never seen since the war began. It had evidence of an absolute victory obtained by the Lord's blessing upon the godly party principally." *Cromwell on the Battle of Marston Moor.*

Above The Battle of Naseby, the last major engagement of the First Civil War.

of praise for his troops. He told the Speaker of the House of Commons: "Honest men served you bravely in the action; sir, they are trusty . . . he that ventures his life for liberty of the country, I wish he trust God for the liberty of his conscience and you for the liberty he fights for."

After Naseby the war was virtually finished, but in places the Royalists still fought on. Cromwell was sent to capture the remaining Royalist strongholds. Most of these were family houses which went into a state of siege rather than surrender. At Bridgewater, Cromwell had

a narrow escape. Mrs Wyndham, the wife of a Royalist commander, fired a cannon at him. Cromwell escaped unhurt, but the man next to him was killed. Mrs Wyndham later sent a message to Cromwell asking him whether he had received her "love token"!

In May 1646 Charles I surrendered to the Scots. In June, Oxford, the last Royalist stronghold, also submitted. This brought an official end to the First Civil War. The end of the war now gave Cromwell a chance to show that his skills were not only confined to the battlefield.

8. Nothing but Confusion

The surrender of Charles I caused a great deal of confusion. The religious and political differences that had caused the war remained unsolved. New problems had also arisen. The two most urgent were: what was going to happen to the New Model Army, and would England adopt the Presbyterian church, according to the Solemn League and Covenant?

The problem which needed an immediate solution was the plight of the Army. The Parliament which assembled in 1646 decided to disband it. This enraged the Army, which had not been paid for several months. They therefore refused to disband until they had been paid. Most of these soldiers were Independents, and were thus against the Covenant, which made their discontent all the more dangerous for Parliament.

Parliament took a very ungrateful attitude towards the Army, which had served it so well. It agreed to grant the men only six weeks' pay, and no more. A General Council of the Army was set up by the "Agitators" to negotiate for full payment. They asked Cromwell to join them, but added rather mysteriously that they were prepared "to go their way without him". Cromwell saw how dangerous a split between the Army and Parliament could be. He tried to calm things down. He warned the soldiers, "If that [Parliament's] authority falls to nothing, nothing but confusion can follow." But the Army was "under a deep sense of

> "As Englishmen ... and surely our being soldiers hath not stripped us of that interest, though our malicious enemies would have it so ... we desire a settlement of the peace of the kingdom and the liberties of the subject, according to the votes and declarations of Parliament, which before we took up arms were by Parliament used as arguments to invite us and divers of our dear friends out ... some of whom have lost their lives in this war." *General Council of the Army, 1646.*

Opposite Cromwell suppressing the mutiny in the Army.

> "After Cromwell quitted the Parliament, his chief dependance was on the Army, which he endeavoured by all means to keep in unity, and if he could not bring it to his sense, he, rather than suffer any division in it, went over himself and carried his friends with him into that way, which the Army did choose." *Sir John Berkely.*

suffering". The more Cromwell tried to please them the more they accused him of betraying them.

Cromwell was also mistrusted by Parliament, who disliked his Independent views. So, not being trusted by either side, Cromwell had to make the difficult decision of which side he was going to support. After much time spent in prayer he threw in his lot with the Army.

Having made up his mind, Cromwell acted with his usual force and determination. He secretly ordered Cornet Joyce to go to Holmby House and capture the King, for he realized that whoever held the King was in the best position for negotiations. Having given these orders, Cromwell left London. This was just as well, for the next day Parliament ordered his arrest. They hoped his imprisonment would end the unrest in the Army.

Not only did Cromwell manage to escape arrest, but the King was brought to him at Newmarket as he had planned. Here Charles was treated with respect by Cromwell and Fairfax, but he refused to negotiate with the "Gentlemen Independents". Instead Charles turned to the Scots.

Parliament was at last concerned. It offered to pay the Army the full amount due. But the Army was no longer interested in just their money. They were after bigger game, for they now wanted a say in how the country was run. In a Declaration issued in June 1647, the Army Council demanded the expulsion of Denzil Holles and the other anti-Army MPs. They also wanted a new election of members. To defend himself and London, Holles raised troops and took over the capital. This violent act horrified many of the more moderate MPs, many of whom sought the protection of the Army.

Cromwell then rode into London at the head of twenty thousand troops. He relieved the capital and Holles was forced to flee. He justified this by saying it was in "the defence of their own and the people's rights and liberties". Although now safe from Parliament, the

Army had new problems. This time the danger came from within its own ranks.

A group known as the Levellers came to the fore. They were led by John Lilburne, who was nicknamed "Free-born John", and wanted power to be in the hands of the ordinary people. In October 1647 they presented their aims in a document known as the Agreement of the People. The ordinary soldiers went wild with delight and wore copies of it in their hats. Cromwell was not so pleased. Outraged at their behaviour, he went among them, drawing his sword and threatening them. One man was actually shot for the part he had played in the affair.

Why was Cromwell's reaction so violent, when he was meant to support his fellow soldiers in all things? He and several other generals felt that the Levellers were trying to "raise the servant against the master". The Levellers, amongst other things, wanted to give every man the vote, and the generals were afraid of giving too much power to the people. Speaking about the Levellers, Cromwell was convinced that "you [the Army Council] have no other way but to break them to pieces . . . if you do not break them, they will break you." The mutinies and revolts inspired by the Levellers were harshly put down.

By ruthlessness and courage, Cromwell had risen to become the champion of the Army in peacetime. Now he had to face the difficult task of coming to some sort of agreement with Charles.

> **"If the master and servant be equal electors, then clearly those that have no interest in the kingdom will make it their interest to choose those that have no interest."** *Colonel Rich on the arguments against the Levellers' proposals.*

9. That Man of Blood

While the Army and Parliament quarrelled, Charles I was busily playing all sides off against each other.

As has been seen, he was kidnapped by the Army and taken to Newmarket, where Cromwell and the other "brutish Generals" had genuinely tried to come to some arrangement that was acceptable to both sides. In 1647 the Heads of Proposals had been put to him. These offered his restoration as king, and allowed for his High Church religion to be practised, provided that it was closely supervised by Parliament. But Charles rejected these proposals, as he had done all others.

Shortly afterwards Charles escaped to the Isle of Wight. Many felt that Cromwell had planned this in order to get him off his hands. But in fact Charles's escape did not make things any easier for Cromwell. By now he realized that further negotiations with the King were impossible. The reason for this was that Charles was secretly negotiating with the Scots. In December 1647 Charles signed what was known as The Engagement. It was a foolish Act and served to harden Cromwell's heart against him.

Up until that time, Cromwell had tried everything to find a solution whereby the King could still retain his position. Now he abandoned all such hope. But his anger was not directed against the monarchy as an institution, but was rather against one man, "that man of blood", Charles Stuart. As on many previous

"We are not traitors, nor murderers, nor fanatics, but Christians and Commonwealth men ... we sought the public good and would have enfranchised the people, and secured the welfare of the whole groaning creation if the nation had not more delight in servitude than freedom." *The Counsel for the Prosecution at the trial of Charles I, 1649.*

Opposite This lifelike painting of Charles I at his execution is by Ernest Crofts, the Victorian battle painter who became keeper of the Royal Academy.

Above Charles at his trial in Westminster Hall, 1649.

occasions, Cromwell sought God in prayer to help him make the right decision. He finally decided that the destruction of Charles I was the only answer left—"if it be an absolute and indisputable necessity for us to do it, then it must be done."

In December a Vote of No Addresses was passed and negotiations with Charles were abandoned. Charles's only hope for survival lay with the Scots and a possible Royalist uprising. In May 1648 the storm Charles had been waiting for broke. There were Royalist uprisings in Wales, Kent, Essex and the North. These were followed by a Scottish uprising.

Cromwell acted instantly. Marching through Wales to Scotland he checked the advance of the Scots. In August the Scots were finally defeated at the Battle of Preston.

Meanwhile, in the South, Fairfax broke the siege of Colchester and restored order there. He then returned to London and, on behalf of the Army, presented a remonstrance to Parliament that "the grand author of all our troubles" be put to trial. At Westminster, all MPs who opposed this trial or who were Presbyterians were forcibly kept out. Forty-five MPs were arrested and ninety-five were excluded. This event is generally known as Pride's Purge—named after the Colonel in charge of the troops. The remaining MPs are generally known as the Rump.

Cromwell was still in the North while all this was going on, but he wrote to say that "he had not been acquainted with these designs but since they were done he was glad of it, and would endeavour to maintain it." He was determined that Charles's trial should be as legal as possible. He was also resolved that Charles should die for the crimes that he had committed. Cromwell looked upon his military victories as a sign that his was God's chosen party. Few were as sure as Cromwell. The two Lord Chief Justices refused to take any part in the trial, so the prosecution had to be carried out by two obscure lawyers. On 20th January, 1649, the trial of King Charles I began in the Court of Justice in Westminster Hall. Of the 135 Members of Parliament Cromwell had bullied into agreeing to appear, only 80 arrived. Even Fairfax refused to come.

Dignified and serene, Charles refused to admit that the court was legal; he laughed when he was called a traitor. Lady Fairfax was less restrained. She cried out "It is a lie . . . Oliver Cromwell is a rogue and a traitor".

On 27th January Charles was found guilty and sentenced to be executed. He was found guilty of being "a tyrant, traitor, murderer and a public and implacable enemy of the commonwealth of England" Cromwell had to use all manner of threats and persuasion to find fifty-five men to sign the death-warrant. But he had no scruples about it, and said "I will cut off his head with the crown on it."

On 30th January, 1649, Charles died calmly and with so much dignity and bravery that he was immediately considered a martyr.

The King was dead. Cromwell thus found himself the most powerful and influential man in England. In many ways it was an unenviable position, for many questions and problems remained unanswered. The next few years were to be a real test of his skill, judgement and strength of character.

> **"The night that King Charles was beheaded my Lord Southampton and a friend . . . got leave to sit up by the body in the Banqueting Hall at Whitehall. As they were sitting very melancholy there, about two o'clock in the morning, they heard the tread of someone coming very slowly upstairs. By and by, the door opened and a man entered, very much muffled up in his cloak and his face quite hid in it. He approached the body, considered it very attentively for some time and then shook his head, sighed out the words 'cruel necessity'. He then departed in the same slow and concealed manner as he came. Lord Southampton used to say that he could not distinguish anything of his face but that by his voice and gait he took him to be Oliver Cromwell."** *Spence*, Anecdotes.

> **"That blood defileth the land, and the land cannot be cleansed of the blood that is shed therein, but by the blood of him that shed it."** *Cromwell on Charles I, 1649.*

10. These Barbarous Wretches

Following the execution of the King, a Council of State was set up to govern the country until some more permanent form of government could be devised. The Council was made up of forty members, most of whom were moderate men. In February 1649 the monarchy and the House of Lords were officially abolished as being "useless, burdensome and dangerous". But the most pressing problem came from Ireland.

The Irish had traditionally been a thorn in England's flesh. In 1641 a serious revolt had broken out and it had been allowed to continue, for neither the King nor Parliament trusted the other with the control of an army to subdue it. On Charles I's death, Ireland refused to acknowledge the Commonwealth. The situation was made even more dangerous by the possibility of Charles Stuart, the dead King's son then in exile in Europe, using Ireland as a base for an invasion of England.

In March 1649 Cromwell was made Commander-in-Chief to lead re-inforcements to restore order to Ireland. As usual he made sure that his troops were well-trained, fed, equipped and paid. In July he sailed for Ireland. Due to the threat of invasion, the campaign had to be quick, efficient and cheap. This is exactly what it was.

Cromwell's first objective was the town of Drogheda, on the mouth of the Boyne. Almost the entire garrison

> "And now the Irish are ashamed
> To see themselves in one year tamed
> So much can one man do
> That doth both act and know."
> *Andrew Marvell.*

Opposite An anti-Catholic engraving, showing Irish Protestants being dragged through bogs and hung on poles by tenterhooks.

of two thousand soldiers and as many civilians were slaughtered by Cromwell's forces. The next town to be put to the sword was Wexford. Here, after an eight-day siege, over three thousand soldiers, priests and civilians were butchered with little or no mercy. His excuse for these atrocities was "to prevent the effusion of blood for the future". By October Cromwell's name was enough to strike terror into Irish hearts.

The campaign went on into the winter, as Cromwell was anxious to have it completed as soon as possible: "We could not keep to the field as we do, were it not we hope to save blood by it . . . in prosecuting the enemies whilst they have the fear of God upon them." But by November, many of the soldiers, including Cromwell himself, were suffering from malaria and dysentery. "There is a considerable part of your army fitter for the hospital than the field," remarked a friend. Cromwell bemoaned the fact that "I scarce have one officer amongst forty that hath not been sick."

In May 1650, however, Cromwell was recalled to England. He left his son-in-law, Henry Ireton, in command, and set sail. Cromwell's campaign in Ireland had been successful. Its effects were devastating and ruthless. Can such slaughter ever be justified? Were Cromwell's deeds as black as his reputation in Ireland?

To begin with, the responsibility does not lie on Cromwell's shoulders alone. To a great extent he was only obeying the orders of the Council of State. Secondly, the Irish had long been hated by the English (and vice versa) and were regarded as little better than animals. Thirdly, they were Roman Catholics; Cromwell, therefore, considered them sinners. Thus, he saw this campaign as a sort of religious crusade. He believed that making the Irish dependant on England could only improve their physical and spiritual well-being.

The campaign was horrible, bloody and ruthless. But any other commander of the period would probably

Left Cromwell at Drogheda, 1649, where almost the entire garrison of four thousand soldiers and civilians were put to the sword.

have acted in the same manner. Cromwell sincerely felt that what he did was for the good of the Irish and that, by acting swiftly, further bloodshed would be avoided. He was convinced that God was behind him the whole way, and that he was God's servant.

In the long run, however, Cromwell's success in Ireland was only on the battlefield. The long-term effects were correctly and ominously outlined by the historian Sir Charles Firth: "Their memory still helps to separate the two races Cromwell wished to unite."

"Our men... were ordered by me to put them all to the sword. And indeed being in the heat of the action, I forbade them spare any that were in the arms of the town, and I think that night they put to the sword about 2,000 men." *Cromwell on Drogheda.*

11. The Crowning Mercy

The reason for Cromwell's recall from Ireland was once again a military one. This time the threat came from Scotland.

The execution of Charles I had horrified Scotland, and the Scots refused to acknowledge the authority of Parliament. In the early months of 1650 the Earl of Montrose, a staunch Royalist, raised a Cavalier army and prepared to invade England in the name of Charles II. However, he was captured by the Covenanters (those who had pledged support to the Presbyterian church) and executed. In May of the same year Charles Stuart himself opened negotiations with the Covenanters and even signed the Covenant. In it he promised to support the Presbyterians if they helped him regain his throne. Both parties agreed to the terms and Charles sailed to Scotland from Holland.

Understandably these events were regarded with alarm in England. The Council of State felt they needed the military advice and experience of their General. Thus Cromwell was recalled. On his return Cromwell found that he was very popular and looked upon as a hero. He was "entertained with many vollies of shot". In turn he was "very affable and courteous".

In June it was decided that Cromwell and Fairfax should take the troops to Scotland. Fairfax was to be in command. When he heard that the intention was actually to invade Scotland he refused to "invade a

> **"It was the visible hand of God, with our own laziness, and not the men that defeated them."** *David Leslie on the Battle of Dunbar, 1650.*

Opposite Cromwell preparing for the Battle of Dunbar, 1650, where he claimed a decisive victory against the Scots.

neighbour nation, especially our brethren of Scotland, to whom we are engaged in Solemn League and Covenant". Cromwell tried to make him change his mind and "laboured it almost all night with earnest endeavours". But all was in vain. Fairfax refused to be swayed, and Cromwell was made Commander-in-Chief. On 4th July, 1650, war was declared on Scotland.

Immediately Cromwell was busy organizing the invasion forces. On the way up to Scotland he was greatly acclaimed and royally entertained with "wyne, biskets, beare and tobacko". Shrewdly Cromwell remarked to a fellow officer, "do not trust that, for those very persons would shout as much if you and I were going to be hanged."

The subduing of the Scots was done in a very different manner from the campaign in Ireland. Because they were fellow Protestants and had been their allies in the Civil Wars, the Scots were felt to be far superior to the "barbaric" Irish. For this reason, Cromwell was reluctant to fight them. He tried first to reason with them, and asked if they could perhaps be mistaken in their views. The Scots were stubborn and refused to listen. In the end the quarrel had to be settled on the battlefield.

On 3rd September the two armies met at Dunbar. Cromwell's opponent was David Leslie, who had been his ally at Marston Moor. The English troops were easily outnumbered. The Scots were confident that the victory was going to be theirs. The night before the battle Cromwell rode among his men, "biting his lips till the blood ran down his chin, without perceiving it, his thoughts being busily employed to be ready for the action now in hand".

It was quality, not quantity, that finally won the day. Cromwell's more experienced and well-disciplined men fought to an overwhelming victory. Even Crom-

"The general himself comes in the rear of our regiment and commands [us] to incline to the left; that was to make more ground to be clear of all the bodies, and so we did, and horse and foot were engaged all over the field, and the Scots all in confusion...the Scots ran and were no more heard of that fight...all our men having chase and execution some eight miles." *A soldier at the Battle of Dunbar, 1650.*

56

well was a little amazed at their good fortune; "the Lord upheld us with comfort in Himself beyond ordinary experience." He also noted, perhaps rather optimistically, that "we lost not above thirty men." The Scots suffered thirty thousand dead and a further ten thousand men were taken prisoner. Although it was a decisive battle, Dunbar solved nothing. The Scots refused to surrender, and in January 1651 Charles Stuart was crowned King Charles II at Scone. Wearily Cromwell confessed "I grow an old man, I feel the infirmities of old age marvellously steal upon me."

For the next five months ill-health and war weariness wore down the English troops. Cromwell fell ill, which prevented the instant completion of the Scottish campaign. The sickness was a recurrence of the malaria which he had picked up in Ireland the year before. It was to prove to be far more than just a passing illness.

In July 1651 the course of events started to quicken up. Charles II led an army down from Stirling into England. He was hoping to persuade Wales and Lancashire to come to his aid. Cromwell, to some extent now recovered, started a skilful series of manoeuvres. By September Charles was surrounded at Worcester. This time the numbers were reversed. Cromwell had 28,000 men, with an extra 5,000 re-inforcements at Coventry. Charles had only 12,000 men, an alarming situation which caused Leslie to remark "he knew well that that army howsoever well they looked would never fight."

But he was proved wrong. On 3rd September, 1651, exactly a year after Dunbar, the Battle of Worcester was fought. Only after a long and bloody struggle did Cromwell again emerge as the victor. "It was", he said, "for aught I know a crowning mercy" and further evidence that he had gained God's approval by "the nation and change of government, by making the people so willing to the defence thereof." Worcester is

Above Charles II's coronation at Scone, 1651.

"I thought I should have died of this fit of sickness, but the Lord seemeth to dispose otherwise... my sickness was so violent that indeed my nature was not able to bear the weight of it." *Cromwell on his bout of malaria, 1651.*

57

often called Cromwell's most brilliant victory. It also marks the end of his military career, and was the last great battle of the Civil Wars.

Once the Scots were defeated, peace terms were drawn up. Cromwell was anxious that the Presbyterian religion should not be harmed. He was, therefore, unwilling to interfere, and in February 1652 negotiations for a union between the two countries began. Although many reforms were carried out, the union did not survive Cromwell's death. As with Ireland, the settlement in Scotland was only temporary and no permanent solution was found.

Right After his defeat at the Battle of Worcester, 1651, Charles II is supposed to have hidden in an oak tree.

12. The Lord hath done with you

Once Ireland and Scotland had been pacified, Cromwell immediately turned to the next urgent problem—the need for a strong and stable government in England.

From the very beginning, Cromwell found himself in a serious dilemma. There was no king, yet he still favoured a monarchy as a means of government. But he also knew that a monarchy would never be accepted by his independent colleagues who had strong Republican views. (These men were in favour of rule by representatives of the nation as a whole, rather than by one person.) For the rest of his life, therefore, Cromwell was to find himself torn between his desire for a traditional solution to the problem and the revolutionary action that was forced on him.

In the first few months of 1649 England was governed by the Council of State and the Rump Parliament. The latter had become very unpopular. A Royalist, George Bate, considered that "the most sordid of men . . . of the vilest condition" had replaced "the most wealthy and grave citizens". Although this is a biased opinion, it was shared by many. Dissatisfaction and grumbles spread that the Rump had done none of the things that it had promised to do. Few reforms of any importance had been passed during their sitting and no future ones seemed to be being discussed.

The Army was anxious for reforms in the areas of the Law, religion and the poor. Cromwell was also keen

> **"How shall we now behave ourselves after such mercies? What is the Lord adoing? What prophecies are now fulfilling? Who is a God like ours?"** *Cromwell to the Rev Cotton of Boston, 1649.*

> **"We were ruled by a King, Lords and Commons; now by a General, a Court Martial and a House of Commons, and we pray what is the difference?"** *John Lilburne, leader of the Levellers.*

Above Another satirical playing card. The caption reads "The Rump and dreggs of the house of Com remaining after the good members were purged out."

that something should be done. He saw that members of the Rump were not up to the task of government, but he did not want to cause any more quarrels. He hoped that the Rump would dissolve itself peacefully. The Army, however, was not content to leave things there. They put so much pressure on Cromwell that in the end he decided that "they [the Rump] should devolve their trust to persons of honour and integrity, that were well-known men well-affected to religion and the interest of the nation." But a new snag appeared in the person of Sir Henry Vane and his supporters. They were a group of MPs who were afraid that the end of the Rump would make way for rule by the Army. They were determined to stay in power. They suggested that a Bill be introduced by which the members of the Rump would keep their seats without re-election, and also have the right to exclude all newly-elected members. (There were many seats vacant due to Pride's Purge.)

This plan was very unpopular with the Army and most of the moderate MPs. After lengthy discussions, Cromwell felt that he had finally persuaded Vane to postpone the bill. He said that it would have created another Rump, only slightly disguised. But the next day Vane opened up further debates on the now forbidden Bill. Cromwell was not in the Commons but Colonel Harrison immediately crept out of the House and ran to fetch him. Cromwell was so furious when he heard the news that he did not even change his thick grey woollen socks. Quickly he gathered together some guards and went straight to the House of Commons. Quietly he took his place inside and said nothing until the Speaker put forward the motion that "this Bill be passed". Then Cromwell stood up and began a long and passionate speech. He talked calmly at first about the Good Old Cause until his temper got the better of him. Marching up and down, flinging his arms in the air, he called the MPs "drunkards" and "whore-masters". Eventually he shouted: "The Lord hath done with you . . . come, come, I will put an end to your prating." Picking up the Mace, the symbol of the Speaker's authority, he cried, "what shall we do with this bauble? Here take it away." He called in twenty musketeers and ordered them to clear the House.

So ended the rule of the Rump. Cromwell told them: "It's you that have forced me to do this, for I sought the Lord day and night, that he would slay me than put me to the doing of this work." The forcible expulsion of the Rump made Cromwell briefly the most popular man in England. No one seemed sorry to see it go. "There was not so much as the barking of a dog or any general or visible repining of it," said the man who threw it out.

> **"The King's head was not taken off because he was king, nor the Lords because they were Lords, but because they did not perform their trust."** *Cromwell in 1653.*

Below Cromwell about to seize the Mace and dissolve the Rump.

13. The Assembly of Saints

Having disposed of the Rump, Cromwell now had to find something to replace it. Plans were discussed for a new parliament, but a free election was definitely out of the question. No-one could be sure that Cromwell and the Generals would be voted back in. A nominated parliament seemed to be the only answer. Cromwell, with "the advice of [the] Council of Officers", selected 140 people from lists of candidates recommended by Presbyterian churches all over the country.

This Parliament is generally known as the Assembly of Saints (all its members were those who "rule[d] in the fear of God"), or Barebones' Parliament (after one of the members whose name was Praise-be-to-God-Barebones). Although some complained that it was made up of "persons of no quality...artificers of the meanest trade", Cromwell had taken pains to ensure that they were all "godly men...fearing God". 129 members came from England, 5 from Scotland and 6 from Ireland. This made it the first parliament of the United Kingdom. Cromwell was very enthusiastic and had great hopes for it: "This may be the door to usher in the things God has promised...you are at the edge of the promises and the prophecies...the poorest Christian, the most mistaken Christian, shall desire to live peaceably and quietly under you...I say, if any desire but lead a life of godliness and honesty, let him be protected."

"And yet, it was done in my simplicity. It was thought then that men of judgment, who had fought in the wars, and were all of a peace upon that account, why surely these men will hit it, and these men will do it to the purpose, whatever can be desired. And such a company of men were chosen and did proceed to action. And this was the naked truth, that the issue was not answerable to the simplicity and honesty of the design." *Cromwell on the failure of the Saints.*

Opposite An engraving of Cromwell as Protector by William Faithorne, who served as a Royalist and was banished for refusing allegiance to Cromwell.

Below John Lilburne (1618–57), leader of the religious group known as the Levellers.

The Saints went to work at an amazing speed. Many reforms were quickly passed: births, deaths and marriages had to be registered; further relief for the poor was granted; punishments were made more humane. Between July and December 1653 eighty Bills were introduced and twenty-six Acts were passed.

However, it did not work. The Saints were as divided in their opinions as the members of the Rump had been. The more conservative men were alarmed at the pace with which some of the bills were dealt with. Cromwell was annoyed that they did not consult him on everything. The Levellers were upset that their leader, John Lilburne, had been imprisoned yet again. The main trouble was that they tried to give the country what they thought it wanted, rather than what it actually needed.

In December 1653 the Assembly of Saints came to an end. The moderates got up early one morning, before the more extreme members had arrived, and voted their own dissolution. Then they went to Cromwell and resigned all their power into his hands. They gave him "power over the three nations, without being a limit set". Cromwell denied having any prior knowledge of this plan, but was prepared to accept it.

The failure of his nominated parliament had a bad effect on Cromwell. Although he tried to put some of the blame on the Army he felt it was the "story of my own folly and weakness". He was afraid that by being so ready to hand over the power given to him by God, he had sinned. From that time onwards, he no longer expected to see the rule of God's People in England. Now he felt that his most important task was to keep the peace. His role became that of a Constable.

As the 1st Earl of Clarendon wrote: "Tired, disillusioned but still passionate in his love of God, Cromwell proceeded with strange dexterity towards reconciling all sorts of people."

14. The Wretched Jealousies

Once again the resignation of the Parliament—the Assembly of Saints—left a void. And once again, having the power of "three nations" in his hands, Cromwell was the man who had to find a replacement.

An immediate plan was presented to him in the form of the Instrument of Government. This was an outline of a constitution designed by John Lambert, and was an attempt to reach a compromise between the Army and Parliament. It is unique in that it was the first written constitution England had ever received. Its most novel idea was the invention of the title of Lord Protector. This position was given to Cromwell for life. In theory, it meant that he would have as much power and authority as a king but under a more acceptable title.

Cromwell was installed as Protector in Westminster Abbey in December 1653. It was a simple ceremony, with Cromwell dressed in black velvet.

To outward appearances the Instrument of Government was a popular move, and for eight months Cromwell and his Council worked smoothly together. They had high hopes for the future. The three kingdoms of Scotland, Ireland and England were officially united —an idea far ahead of its time. Religion was taught throughout the country and preachers were encouraged. Grants were made to schools and higher education was allowed to develop. Durham University was founded and grants of money were given to the universities of Oxford and Glasgow.

> **"A new militia, raised with a tendency to divide this country into provinces, a power too great to be bound by any law; in plain terms to cantonize the nation."**
> *Contemporary view on the Protectorate and the Major-Generals. ("Cantonize" means to divide for military purposes.)*

Statue of Oliver Cromwell by
M. Noble.

In September 1654 the First Parliament of the Protectorate was summoned. It was called according to the rules laid down in the Instrument of Government. It was fairly elected, except that Roman Catholics and known Royalists were excluded. Cromwell was again full of enthusiasm for this Parliament, which shows that all his hopes cannot have been dashed by the failure of the Assembly of Saints. "Gentlemen, you are met here on the greatest occasion that I believe England ever saw; having upon your shoulders the interests of three nations." He urged them to "a sweet, gracious and holy understanding of one and other and of your business". But Cromwell was to be disappointed once again. The radicals, led by his old enemy Sir Henry Vane, immediately questioned the legality of the Instrument to summon a parliament. They also objected to Cromwell having such extensive king-like powers. Another sore point was that Cromwell also controlled the Army, and Vane felt that this should have been Parliament's responsibility. Cromwell defended himself by saying that he had accepted the title of Lord Protector in order to achieve a "healing and settling" at home, as well as for peace and security abroad.

But Vane, together with his friend Haslerigg, refused to listen. They started to draw up their own constitution. They had over ninety supporters. Afraid of disorder in the country, Cromwell took strong measures to suppress them. He surrounded Parliament with guards and then treated the Commons to one of his long passionate speeches. He told them that they must accept government by one person and made them promise to be loyal to the Protectorate. 300 out of the 410 swore loyalty. The Republicans refused and left the House. Cromwell waited until the five months' compulsory period of sitting for a parliament were up, and then dissolved the still turbulent members.

An important split had now developed in Parliament

Above Major-General John Lambert.

Below Sir Henry Vane.

which seriously disturbed Cromwell's hoped-for peace and security. To add to these troubles a rebellion had broken out. The Royalists, taking advantage of the quarrels in parliament, had risen in Wiltshire, Berkshire and Dorset. This is generally known as Pennruddock's Rising. Although it was not serious and was easily subdued, the rebellion showed that stricter control was needed over the counties. Cromwell's next scheme was designed to deal with that problem. He decided to divide England into eleven areas, each one to be looked after by a Major-General. This was the high point of Cromwell's use of military power to secure authority. The Major-Generals were put in control of the militia and ordered to enforce rigorously a strict puritan way of life. It was at this time that such entertainments as drinking, dancing, gambling and singing (other than hymns) were forbidden and throughout the country theatres were closed. The Sabbath was very strictly observed and life was made as spartan and "pure" as possible. Needless to say, the Major-Generals were very unpopular and were greatly disliked. They were further resented as a tax was levied on all property to finance their upkeep. The local gentry and Justices of the Peace were upset at having their jobs taken from them.

In the spring of 1657 the Second Parliament of the Protectorate was summoned. It was chiefly called to finance the Spanish war, which had broken out the year before, but it was also used as an opportunity of getting rid of the Major-Generals.

Cromwell was bitterly disappointed and disillusioned by the failure of yet another of his schemes. He found himself deserted by many of his old friends, unable to reconcile the Royalists and with no settled form of government. As he said to his son-in-law Charles Fleetwood: "The wretched jealousies that are amongst us and the spirit of calumny turn all into gall and wormwood."

Opposite This cartoon of "Cromwell's car" shows the wheels going over Charles I. In the balance Cromwell holds liberty and religion, and the sleeping ladies with crowns represent England, Scotland and Ireland.

68

15. The Glory he had abroad

While Cromwell's schemes for a stable government at home were not proving successful, the situation abroad looked far more promising. Clarendon considered that: "Cromwell's greatness at home was but a shadow of the glory he had abroad."

Basically there were three aims which governed Cromwell's foreign policy. Firstly, he wanted to "set England at the head of the Protestant cause in Europe". (Both France and Spain, the two major European powers, were Catholic.) Secondly, he wanted to make sure that Charles II could not get foreign aid to help him invade England. Thirdly, he hoped to promote English trade. These aims were hindered and sometimes helped by international disagreements.

The first signs of trouble came from Holland. The Dutch were not one of England's traditional enemies (unlike France and Spain), but between 1652–54 England was at war with them. It was an important war because it was fought over trade rights and not religion. The main cause was commercial jealousy. In 1651 England had passed a Navigation Act which forbade the importation of any goods into England except by English ships, or by ships belonging to the country which produced the goods. It crippled the Dutch, who enjoyed a large part of the carrying trade. But the Dutch in turn had signed a treaty with Denmark which had ruined English trade in the Baltic.

> **"God hath brought us hither to consider the work we may do in the World, as well as at home."** *Cromwell.*

Opposite Admiral Robert Blake, who led the English fleet in the Dutch and Spanish wars, keeping discipline aboard his ship.

Right The Dutch fleet defeated by Admiral Blake off Portland in 1653.

Cromwell was not pleased by the course that events were taking: "I do not like the war, I will do everything in my power to bring about peace." But on the whole the war went well for England, who had the advantages of a good Admiral, Robert Blake, and a greatly improved fleet. But in November 1652 the English, under Blake, were defeated off Dungeness by the Dutch Admiral Van Tromp. In February 1653, however, the Dutch were beaten off Portland. It was an expensive

war, and it had broken out at a time of great difficulty
at home. From the beginning Cromwell had been
negotiating for peace. In April 1654 peace was con-
cluded when the Treaty of Westminster was signed. The
terms secured English trade and supremacy in English
waters. In the treaty the Dutch promised not to help
Charles II or protect any Royalists seeking refuge in
Holland. They also promised to pay honour to the
flag of the Commonwealth on the sea and to make

compensation for damage done to English merchants. To make English trade safe in other parts of Europe treaties were arranged with other countries. In April 1654 a treaty was signed with Sweden. In the same year Portugal and Denmark also signed treaties. These brought commercial advantages, security against a Royalist invasion and safeguarded the "Protestant interest abroad".

But Cromwell's main hopes lay further afield. He wanted to attack the Spanish possessions in the West Indies and transform them into Protestant colonies. Plans for this were discussed in June 1654, and Cromwell was full of "boastful enthusiasm". In August arrangements were made for the expedition. It finally set sail in December.

It seems to have been doomed from the start. The two Commanders, General Robert Venables and Admiral William Penn, could not see eye to eye about anything. The soldiers were "a gang of common cheats, thieves, cutpurses and such-like persons". There were no proper supplies and few arms. But as usual, Cromwell was confident. He wished them "happy gales and prosperous success to the great enterprise you have in hand".

Arriving in the West Indies, attempts were made to take the islands of Barbados, St Kitts and Hispaniola. These attempts were badly organized. Many men were killed, either in battle or from tropical diseases. When Cromwell heard of their misfortune he flew into "violent distempers". In fact this expedition caused so much dissatisfaction that its leaders were imprisoned on their return to England. Jamaica was the next objective. It was a fertile island with a small population—an ideal place to start a colony. The expedition landed in May 1655. A week later the island surrendered. The victory, however, was overshadowed by the dreadful sufferings of the troops. Out of the original seven thousand over half died, mainly from disease.

Below Admiral William Penn. His attempts to form Protestant colonies in the New World were not so successful, but his son founded Pennsylvania.

Looking on the bright side, Jamaica did now belong to England. Tempting offers were made to persuade people to settle there. Every male over the age of twelve would be given twenty acres (eight hectares) of land, and every female would get ten acres (four hectares). But few people were prepared to go. Cromwell even considered importing some Irish people to populate his colony. In 1656 the affairs of the island were put in the hands of a committee for "His Highness in Jamaica and the West Indies".

Naturally these events had not pleased Spain. In October 1655 war was declared. Again England was very fortunate. In 1656 Blake captured a hoard of silver from a Spanish treasure ship off Cadiz. Then in 1657 France joined the war on the English side. This, according to John Thurloe, Cromwell's secretary, was "a bridle to the Dutch and a door into the Continent". This alliance destroyed the Spanish troops in the Netherlands and gave England Dunkirk. In April 1657 a Spanish fleet was destroyed by Admiral Blake in the Bay of Santa Cruz in Teneriffe. In the following year the Spanish were again defeated at the Battle of the Dunes. The naval historian Michael Lewis considers that for England "this marked an essential step towards sea power and the command of wide stretches of sea."

When Cromwell was born England had only one colony—Virginia. During the Interregnum she gained Jamaica, St Helena, Nova Scotia, New Brunswick and Dunkirk. This was made possible by Cromwell's far-sighted foreign policy and an extension of the Navy (between 1655–60 two hundred ships were built). Clarendon wrote that Cromwell's foreign policy was "magnanimous, enterprising and successful". Europe regarded him with terror and admiration. Under Cromwell England rose to become a dominant sea power and the foundations were laid for the future British Empire.

> "It may be we have not (as the World terms it) been so fortunate in all our successes. Truly, if we have that mind, that God may not determine us in these things, I think we shall quarrel at that which God will answer." *Cromwell after the Hispaniola failure.*

16. The Lord Protector

Two events at the end of 1656 caused national concern. They briefly united the quarrelling Parliament, Army and their Protector.

In December 1656 a Quaker called James Naylor proclaimed that he was the Messiah. He rode through the streets of Bristol on a donkey, imitating Christ on Palm Sunday. He was a religious fanatic, and was probably quite insane. Most people were horrified by his behaviour. He was whipped, branded and imprisoned by order of Parliament. It was a savage sentence. Cromwell had tried to intervene to obtain a lighter punishment but Parliament refused to listen. As a result many people started to think that there should once again be another House to check or approve the actions of the Commons.

In January 1657 an attempt was made to assassinate Cromwell. The attempt became known as Sindercombe's Plot, after the would-be assassin Miles Sindercombe. His actions made Parliament realize how important a figure the Protector was to the peace of the country. As a vote of confidence they gave Cromwell funds for the Spanish war. They also presented him with the Humble Petition and Advice. This document offered Cromwell the crown of England and the power to nominate his successor. It also advised the forming of a "Second House of Parliament". This practically restored the ancient Constitution of the country, and

Above John Naylor in the pillory having his tongue cut out. He claimed to be the Messiah.

Opposite Cromwell invested as Lord Protector in Westminster Abbey, 1567.

Above The Great Seal used during the Protectorate.

gave to Cromwell all the powers belonging to the Sovereign.

Cromwell's answer was perhaps as expected; "I am ready to serve not as a king, but as a constable...a good constable to keep the peace of the parish." He declined the offer, as he could not "find it his duty to God and Parliament to undertake this charge under that title". He also knew that the Army still objected to the title of King. But Parliament refused to give up their idea. The question of who should succeed Cromwell loomed darkly in the minds of many. In May 1657 a second petition was presented to Cromwell. It was almost the same as the first but it omitted the title of King. After much soul-searching Cromwell accepted it. There was a mixed reaction to the news. Cromwell himself said it was but "a feather in a cap". The soldiers felt it was "a fearful Hypocrisy". Others believed that "the things provided in the petition do secure the liberties of God so as they never before had them". On 25th May Cromwell was invested as Lord Protector in Westminster Abbey. This time he was lavishly adorned in purple velvet and ermine.

Cromwell now had the right to name his successor, which would hopefully ensure a peaceful succession at his death. He could also appoint a Second House. This was formed in February 1658 and contained sixty members. Only six of the ancient peers were summoned, and only one of these took his seat. The Third Parliament of the Protectorate refused to acknowledge the "Other House" as they called it. They accused Cromwell of deserting the Good Old Cause. Quarrelling then broke out. It became so violent that Cromwell dissolved his Parliament in fury after it had sat for only sixteen days. When Fleetwood tried to stop him, Cromwell rudely retorted: "You are a milksop, by the living God, I will dissolve this parliament."

The Army was delighted by his actions. A great feast

was held to celebrate. All the officers promised to "stand and fall, live and die with my Lord Protector". The MPs were not silenced, but Cromwell had seen the last of his parliaments, and for the remainder of his life ruled alone.

By 1658 Cromwell was an old man. The anxieties of his position had affected his health. The failure of so many of his dreams had left him disillusioned. The "bastard tertian ague" gnawed at him constantly. This was the old malaria that he had picked up in the Irish bogs in 1649. The fears of a Royalist invasion and the responsibilities of government, together with his bad health, hung heavily on him.

In August his condition grew worse. George Fox, the

Above The death of Oliver Cromwell as visualized by the Victorian painter Wynfield.

> "He's a traitor helps a
>   traitor to the throne,
> Yet who resists him on it
>   may be one."
> *A Royalist poet, 1658.*

79

Opposite Cromwell's head, which stayed on a pole above Westminster Hall during Charles II's reign.

Below "Tumbledown Dick", Cromwell's son Richard.

Quaker, met him in Hampton Court and described how he felt "a waft of death go forth against [me] ... he looked like a dead man". On 24th August prayers were said for him throughout the country. On 30th August a terrible storm racked England. On 3rd September, the anniversary of his two great victories of Dunbar and Worcester, Cromwell died.

> Tossed in a furious hurricane
> Did Oliver give up his reign. (Samuel Butler)

Cromwell felt no regrets at dying. His last words were: "It is not my design to drink or sleep but ... to make what haste I can to be gone."

Cromwell lay in state for eight weeks at Somerset House. Here "multitudes daily crowd[ed] to see this glorious but mournful sight." On 10th November he was buried secretly in the Henry VII Chapel in Westminster Abbey. He "lay among kings and with a more than regal solemnity". On 23rd November he was given an elaborate state funeral. The diarist Evelyn sourly remarked that "it was the joyfullest funeral I ever saw, for there were none that cried but dogs."

Cromwell's son, Richard—"Tumbledown Dick"—was installed as the new Protector. He was not up to the task of government and, not being a soldier, was unpopular with the Army. He soon resigned and retired into private life. Thus the Commonwealth virtually crumbled with its creator. On 30th May, 1660, Charles II returned to "claim his throne".

There is a grotesque finale to the story. In January 1661 the bodies of Cromwell and other prominent Commonwealth men who were responsible for the execution of Charles I were dug up from their graves. Their remains were taken to Tyburn and hung on the gibbet. Cromwell's head was severed and placed on a pole above Westminster Hall. It remained there for the rest of Charles II's reign.

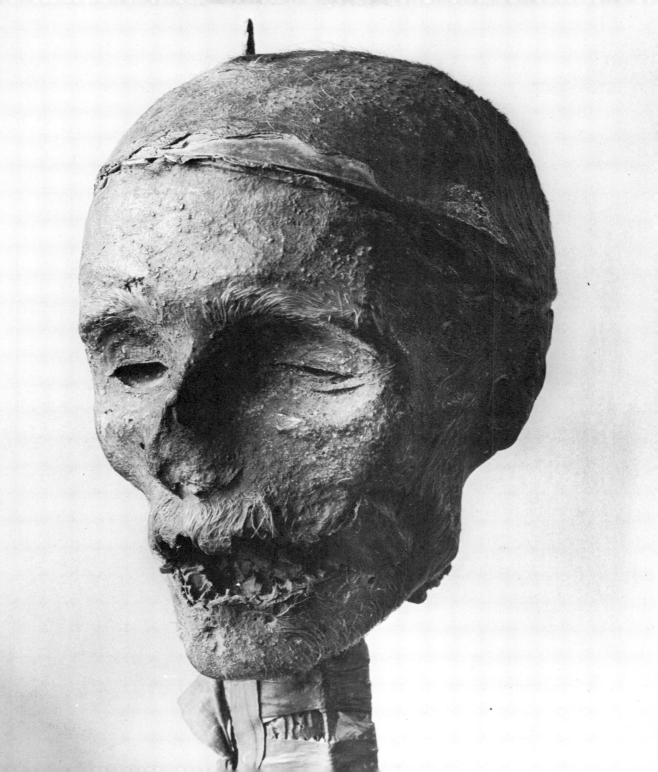

17. God's Chosen Englishman

Cromwell is now recognized as being one of the greatest personalities of English history. For part of his life and for literally hundreds of years after his death, many regarded him as being evil, a blot upon England's past, a murderer of kings. Today he is seen as having been an extraordinary man of outstanding achievements.

Cromwell's rise to power was unique. In the space of fifteen years he rose from an insignificant back-bencher to become a king in all but name. What were his achievements? Was he of any real benefit to England?

Cromwell was one of the most brilliant military leaders ever to emerge in England. This genius is made even more startling by the fact that he had no military training whatsoever. In this area he took a completely new look at the Army. He got rid of all those commanders who owed their position to money rather than skill. His caring attitude towards his troops brought its own rewards, as can be seen by the calibre of his famous Ironsides. Cromwell's foreign policy was sound and, on the whole, successful, for he laid the foundations for the future British Empire. Cromwell caused England to be both admired and feared.

At home his policies were generally less successful. But the problems that he faced were not only enormous but also had never been faced before. The execution of the King and the abolition of the House of Lords left

> "Oliver Cromwell lay buried and dead
> Heigho, buried and dead;
> There grew a green apple tree over his head
> Heigho, over his head;
> The apples were ripe and ready to drop
> Heigho...
> Oliver rose and gave her a crack
> That knocked the old woman flat on her back.
> The apples were dried and they lie on the shelf
> If you want one you must get it yourself."
> *Old nursery rhyme.*

Opposite Charles II returning to London to claim his throne.

the country in a unique position. For any one man to devise a workable form of government that was acceptable to all the many warring factions remaining after the Civil War was a task of Herculean proportions. The fact that Cromwell was able to rule a country so recently torn apart by a bitter and bloody war when he had no experience of such power, was a tremendous achievement in itself. The five years of the Protectorate gave peace and security to England after an extremely unstable and restless period. There was no great massacre of known Royalist supporters. There was even a certain amount of religious toleration; for example, Jews were encouraged to settle in England. The penal system was reformed. The arts were encouraged. Portrait painters such as Peter Lely, Peter Walker and Samuel Cooper blossomed. Music also flourished. The first English opera— *The Siege of Rhodes* by D'Avenant—was written during the Interregnum. Education received direct help and new universities were built. Thus it seems that the years of the Protectorate were far from sterile and insignificant.

These changes were primarily due to Cromwell. His reforming zeal was consistent. This was due to his enormous strength of character. His apparent failure with one type of parliament never prevented him from trying again with another in order to find the right formula for successful government. He constantly sought God's guidance and advice in prayer. His belief that he was one of the chosen never left him, and it was this belief that he was doing God's will which ruled all his actions.

Fame and power seemed hardly to have changed him. Extremely ruthless and determined when necessary, Cromwell never lost his tolerance, humility or sincerity. Above all, he remained devoted to his family and to God.

But Cromwell was the Commonwealth. After his

death it died with him, as there was no-one of comparable strength of character or ability to take over. Charles II was welcomed back with great delight and enthusiasm. Lord Shelburne wrote this of Cromwell in 1785: "While he [Cromwell] had power...[he] did more set things forward than all the Kings who reigned during that century.... England was never so much respected abroad, while at home...talents of every kind began to show themselves, which were immediately put to sleep or crushed at the Restoration."

Below Cromwell and his family listening to Milton the blind poet playing the organ.

Principal
Characters

FAIRFAX, SIR THOMAS (1612–71). During the Civil Wars he joined Parliament as a General of Horse. He became the supreme commander of the New Model Army. In 1650 he refused to invade Scotland and his command was taken over by Cromwell. On Cromwell's death he worked for the Restoration of Charles II.

HAMPDEN, JOHN (1594–1643). A Buckinghamshire squire, he entered Parliament in 1621. He was one of the five members Charles I tried to arrest in 1642. He was most renowned for refusing to pay Ship Money in 1637. He was mortally wounded at the Battle of Chalgrove Field in the Civil Wars.

HASLERIGG, SIR ARTHUR (d. 1661). A leading member of the House of Commons, one of the five MPs Charles I attempted to arrest in 1642. He turned against Cromwell in 1653, when the latter accepted the Instrument of Government. He opposed the creation of a second house in 1656.

HOLLES, DENZIL (1599–1680). One of the five members involved in the celebrated case of 1642. He was hostile to Cromwell from the start and spread stories of his cowardice on the battlefield. He was a devout Presbyterian.

IRETON, SIR HENRY (1611–51). A General of the Parliamentary Army during the Civil Wars and husband of Cromwell's daughter, Bridget. He was among those who signed the death warrant of Charles I.

LAUD, WILLIAM (1573–1645). In 1633 he was made Archbishop of Canterbury. With Strafford, Laud developed a system of government which would allow Charles I to rule without Parliament. He supported the High Church religion and believed in the "beauty of Holiness". Along with Charles, he was responsible for the Bishops' Wars, 1639–40. He was hated by the Puritans. In 1640 he was accused of treason and imprisoned in the Tower. He was executed in 1645 for attempting to overthrow Protestantism.

LESLIE, DAVID (1601–82). Commander of the Scottish army. After the Solemn League and Covenant of 1643 he was Parliament's ally. Scots aid was one of the factors which contributed to the victory of Marston Moor in 1644. In 1650 the Scots refused to acknowledge the Commonwealth and Leslie commanded an army in favour of Charles II; he was defeated at Dunbar.

LILBURNE, JOHN (1614–57). Agitator and leader of the Levellers. Nicknamed "Freeborn John", he was frequently imprisoned for his activities and considered by the Generals as dangerous.

MONTAGU, EDWARD, 2ND EARL OF MANCHESTER (1602–71). He was made Commander-in-Chief of the Parliamentarian army. Always a Royalist at heart, he was appalled at the idea of fighting the King. In 1643 he was given the command of the Eastern Association but was forced to resign after the Self-Denying Ordinance.

PYM, JOHN (1584–1643). Entered Parliament in 1614. He was a leading figure of the Long Parliament and attacked the King's misrule. He was nicknamed "King Pym". He was one of the five members whom Charles I tried to arrest in 1642.

WENTWORTH, THOMAS, 1ST EARL OF STRAFFORD (1593–1641). In 1633 he was made Lord Deputy of Ireland,

and by 1640 was one of Charles I's chief advisers. He was disliked by the Puritans and in 1640 was impeached by the House of Commons. He was accused of High Treason and executed upon a Bill of Attainder in the same year. He did not deserve his nickname of "Black Tom Tyrant".

Table of Dates

1599	April	Oliver Cromwell born in Huntingdon, England.
1603		Accession of James I.
1604		Cromwell goes to the free school of Huntingdon.
1616		Cromwell goes to Sidney Sussex College, Cambridge.
1620		Cromwell studies law at Lincoln's Inn Fields. Marries Elizabeth Bouchier.

	Marries	Marries Elizabeth Bouchier
1625		Accession of Charles I.
1628		Cromwell elected Member of Parliament for Huntingdon.
1629		Start of the "Eleven Years Tyranny".
1631		Cromwell's family moves to St Ives.
1636		Cromwell's family moves to Ely.
1637		Ship Money Case.
1638		First Bishops' War.
1640	April–May	Short Parliament.
	November	Long Parliament. Cromwell sits as Member for Cambridge in both.
1641		Execution of the Earl of Strafford. Grand Remonstrance.
1642		Case of the Five Members.
	August	Civil War declared.
	October	Battle of Edgehill.
1643		Cromwell made a Colonel in the Eastern Association.
	September	Solemn League and Covenant.
	October	Battle of Winceby.
1644		Cromwell made Lieutenant-General
	July	Battle of Marston Moor.
	December	Self-Denying Ordinance.
1645		Archbishop Laud executed.
	June	Battle of Naseby.
1646	April	Surrender of Charles I to the Scots.
1647		Heads of Proposals. Agreement of the People.
1648	January	Vote of No Further Addresses.
	April	Second Civil War.
	December	Pride's Purge.

1649	January	Trial and Execution of Charles I. Cromwell made Lord-Lieutenant.
		Subduing of Ireland.
1650		War with Scotland.
	September	Battle of Dunbar.
1651		Charles II crowned in Scotland.
	September	Battle of Worcester.
1652	April	Outbreak of First Dutch War.
1653	April	Dissolution of the Rump.
	July	The Assembly of Saints.
	December	Cromwell becomes Protector.
1654	September	First Parliament of the Protectorate.
	December	Expedition to the West Indies.
1655	March	Pennruddock's rising.
		Seizure of Jamaica.
	August	Rule of the Major-Generals begins.
1656		Second Parliament of the Protectorate.
		Sindercombe's Plot.
1657	May	Humble Petition and Advice.
	June	Cromwell becomes Lord Protector
1658	3rd September	Death of Oliver Cromwell.
		Succession of Richard Cromwell as Lord Protector.
1660	May	Restoration of the Monarchy. Accession of Charles II.

Glossary

BISHOPS' WARS (1639–40). These were two "wars" fought in resistance to Charles I's attempts to introduce the English Prayer Book into Scotland. The Scots were firm Presbyterians and whole congregations walked out of churches, rather than listen to the Prayer Book being read. The Scots were prepared to fight for their religion and raised an army. The First Bishops' War was ended by the Treaty of Berwick. Charles refused to give up his plans until the Scots actually marched down into England. The Second Bishops' War was ended by the Treaty of Ripon in 1640.

GRAND REMONSTRANCE (1641). This was a long list of 204 clauses drawn up by Parliament of all the wrongs suffered by the nation during the reign of Charles I. It also set out all the good work that Parliament had done and contained suggestions for reforms. It was drawn up because the Commons saw that the King was regaining his popularity.

HEADS OF PROPOSALS (July 1646). This was intended as a basis of discussion between the King, the Army and Parliament. It was meant to appeal to all sides but Charles refused to listen. It offered him restoration to his throne and a national Anglican Church, under Parliamentary supervision.

HUMBLE PETITION AND ADVICE (February 1657). This was a revised constitution to replace the Instrument of Government. It offered the crown to Cromwell and suggested the revival of a second House of Parliament. Cromwell refused the first petition but accepted the second, which omitted the title of King. Instead he was given the title of Lord Protector, which was hereditary and more popular with the Army.

LEVELLERS. These were a group of extreme radicals, led by John Lilburne. They were anxious for social reform and believed in government by the ordinary people. They presented a plan for a new constitution in the Agreement of the People. Cromwell and other officers felt that the Levellers were potentially very dangerous and made every effort to curb them. They received most of their support amongst the ordinary soldiers in the Army.

INSTRUMENT OF GOVERNMENT (1653). This was a written constitution drawn up by John Lambert. It made Cromwell Protector for life and gave the office power equal to that of a king. The Protector was to be assisted by a Council of State. It also redistributed the franchise so that people in the newly developing towns were given the vote. Parliament was to meet at least once every three years and was to sit for no less than five months. Religious toleration was guaranteed. The Instrument was used until it was replaced by the Humble Petition and Advice of 1657.

PRESBYTERIANISM. This was a rigid church system. The Presbyterians were so called because they were governed by Presbyters, or Elders, and not by Bishops. It was opposed by the Independents, who were in favour of a more personal religion. They did not want to be told how to worship, but preferred to act according to their consciences. This individuality led to the development of smaller sects being formed, each with their own beliefs. These included the Levellers, Quakers, Anabaptists and Fifth Monarchists.

PRIDE'S PURGE (December 1649). This was the arrest and forcible expulsion of all MPs who were likely to oppose the trial of Charles I. It was conducted by Colonel Pride. Those who remained sitting in Parliament were nicknamed the Rump.

SELF-DENYING ORDINANCE (December 1644). This was the ultimate result of the quarrel between Cromwell and the Earl of Manchester. It forbade all Members of Parliament to have a commission in the forces. This made way for commands being issued to men with military skill rather than social position and money.

SHIP MONEY CASE (1637). The King had an ancient right to demand money for the building of ships from ports and coastal towns in time of war. This was to contribute to the defence of the nation. In 1635, however, Charles I extended the demand to the whole country. This was very unpopular, for there was no danger from war and Charles had demanded it without reference to Parliament. In 1637 John Hampden refused to pay the sum demanded. He said it was an illegal tax as it did not have Parliament's authority. This developed into a court case of Hampden v Rex. Charles won the case but by such a narrow margin that many felt the victory in fact went to Hampden.

SOLEMN LEAGUE AND COVENANT (September 1643). This was a pact between Parliament and the Scots. In return for Scottish troops Parliament agreed to adopt the Presbyterian Church, on winning the war. It was not a completely popular treaty, for many disliked the rigidity of the Presbyterian Church system. In the end a clause was inserted which made it possible to interpret the religious clause more generally.

Further Reading

The Early Stuarts 1603–60 by Godfrey Davies (Oxford University Press, 1959). Clearly presented and easy to understand.

The Century of Revolution 1603–1714 by Christopher Hill (Nelson, 1961; Sphere, 1969). Useful background information for older readers.

God's Englishman: Oliver Cromwell and the English Revolution by Christopher Hill (Weidenfeld and Nicolson, 1970; Penguin, 1972). Valuable for serious students of Cromwell.

Oliver Cromwell by C. V. Wedgwood (Duckworth, 1973). Informative and very useful.

The King's War 1641–47 by C. V. Wedgwood (Collins, 1958; Fontana, 1966). Excellent background on the civil war period, particularly for serious students.

Cromwell, Our Chief of Men by Antonia Fraser (Weidenfeld and Nicholson, 1973; Panther, 1975). Concise, absorbing and very detailed. Recommended for older readers.

Index

Picture Credits

The author and publishers wish to thank all those who have given permission for the reproduction of copyright illustrations on the following pages: Mary Evans Picture Library, *frontispiece*, 12, 16, 26, 31, 35, 36, 40–41, 50, 54, 58, 61, 66, 67a, 72–73, 80, 82; The Radio Times Hulton Picture Library, 10–11, 32, 70, 79, 85; The Mansell Collection, 24, 46, 53, 76; National Portrait Gallery, 28; Sidney Sussex College, 81.